Fact #1: The Berry Paradox

At first glance, one might easily assume that strawberries, with their red, seeded exteriors, qualify as berries, while bananas, with their distinct shape and peel, do not. Yet, the botanical definition turns this common assumption on its head, presenting a fascinating paradox in the fruit world.

In botanical terms, a berry is defined as a simple fruit with seeds and pulp produced from the ovary of a single flower. It is also fleshy throughout, including the innermost part. This definition categorizes bananas as true berries because they stem from a single ovary and contain multiple seeds embedded within their fleshy part. On the other hand, strawberries come from a flower with multiple ovaries, making them aggregate fruits, not berries. This classification highlights the complexity and often counterintuitive nature of botanical nomenclature, challenging our everyday understanding of fruit.

Interesting Tidbit:

The banana plant is often mistaken for a tree; however, it's technically a large herb. The "tree" is actually a pseudostem formed by tightly packed leaf sheaths. Adding to the intrigue, what we commonly refer to as banana "seeds" are the small black specks found in the fruit's centre, but the cultivated varieties are mostly seedless; the seeds have been reduced to these tiny specks due to selective breeding.

Fact #2: Venusian Peculiarities

Venus, our neighbouring planet, presents a curious case where the length of a single day surpasses that of an entire year. This anomaly offers a glimpse into the complex and varied dynamics of planetary rotations and orbits within our solar system.

Venus rotates on its axis at an exceedingly slow pace and in the opposite direction to most planets in the solar system, a phenomenon known as retrograde rotation. It takes about 243 Earth days for Venus to complete one full rotation on its axis, making a Venusian day longer than a Venusian year, which is about 225 Earth days. This slow rotation is in stark contrast to its relatively quick orbit around the Sun, leading to the peculiar circumstance where days outlast years. The reasons behind Venus's slow and retrograde rotation are still a topic of research, with hypotheses suggesting significant asteroid impacts or complex atmospheric dynamics as possible explanations.

Interesting Tidbit:

Despite its leisurely rotation, Venus boasts the most circular orbit of any planet in our solar system, maintaining a nearly perfect circular path around the Sun. Additionally, if you were to stand on Venus's surface, you would experience sunrises in the west and sunsets in the east, contrary to what we experience on Earth, due to its retrograde rotation.

Fact #3: The Immortality of Honey

Honey, known for its delightful sweetness, hides an extraordinary secret within its golden depths – it is one of the few substances on Earth that can last indefinitely without spoiling. This remarkable feature of honey has fascinated humans for centuries, with its preservation properties being as impressive as its taste.

The secret behind honey's eternal shelf life lies in its unique composition and the process by which bees make it. Honey is primarily sugar, and its high sugar content means that it's a highly inhospitable environment for bacteria or microorganisms to grow. Additionally, bees add an enzyme, glucose oxidase, to it. This enzyme breaks down the sugars into gluconic acid and hydrogen peroxide, the latter of which serves as a potent preservative. Furthermore, the low moisture content in honey and its acidic pH level contribute to its long-lasting nature. These factors combined create a natural product that,

when sealed properly, can withstand the test of
time, remaining edible and delicious for
thousands of years.

Interesting Tidbit:

Archaeologists have discovered pots of honey in
ancient Egyptian tombs that are over 3,000
years old, and remarkably, the honey is still
considered edible. This discovery not only
highlights honey's incredible shelf life but also
provides insight into the ancient civilizations' use
of honey for its medicinal and preservative
properties.

Fact #4: The Heart Trio of the Octopus

The octopus, a marvel of the marine world, not only captivates with its intelligence and camouflage skills but also boasts an extraordinary physiological feature: three hearts. This unique trait underscores the complexity and adaptability of octopus biology.

An octopus's circulatory system is quite distinct from that of humans and other terrestrial animals. Two of its hearts, known as branchial hearts, are dedicated to pumping blood through each of the two gills, while the third heart, the systemic heart, pumps oxygenated blood to the rest of the body. This division of labor among the hearts allows the octopus to efficiently oxygenate its blood and maintain its metabolic needs. However, when the octopus swims, the systemic heart stops beating, which explains why these creatures prefer to crawl rather than swim; swimming can exhaust them quickly. The presence of copper-based hemocyanin for transporting oxygen, instead of the iron-based hemoglobin found in mammals, gives their blood a blue colour and supports efficient oxygen transportation in cold ocean environments.

Interesting Tidbit:

Despite their fascinating cardiovascular system, octopuses have relatively short lifespans, often ranging from six months to a few years, depending on the species. The end of life for many male octopuses comes soon after mating, while females typically die shortly after their eggs hatch, a testament to the intense lifecycle and reproductive habits of these creatures.

Fact #5: The Shuffle's Infinite Dance

The simple act of shuffling a deck of cards yields a staggering number of possible outcomes, far exceeding the imagination. This fact delves into the sheer scale of permutations within a standard deck, revealing a complexity that transcends the atomic scale of our planet.

When you shuffle a standard 52-card deck, the number of possible arrangements is calculated by factorial 52 (denoted as 52!), which is 52 x 51 x 50... down to 1. This calculation's results in approximately 8.06×10^{67} different possible sequences. To put this astronomical figure into perspective, it vastly outnumbers the estimated total of atoms on Earth, which is about 1.33×10^{50}. This means that every time you shuffle a deck of cards, it's almost certain that you're holding a sequence of cards that has never existed before in the history of the universe. This mind-boggling fact highlights the incredible diversity and unpredictability contained in the seemingly mundane task of shuffling cards.

Interesting Tidbit:

If every person on Earth (~7.8 billion people) shuffled a unique deck of cards every second since the beginning of the universe (about 13.8 billion years ago), we wouldn't even come close to covering all the possible permutations. This exemplifies not only the vastness of mathematical permutations but also the concept of infinity in a tangible form.

Fact #6: The Triple Point Phenomenon

Water, the most familiar of substances, holds mysteries that defy our everyday experiences with liquids, solids, and gases. Among these is the ability to boil and freeze simultaneously, a rare and intriguing state known as the triple point.

The triple point of water is a specific condition where temperature and pressure are just right for water to exist in all three phases: solid, liquid, and gas, simultaneously. This occurs at precisely 0.01 degrees Celsius (32.018 degrees Fahrenheit) and 611.657 pascals of pressure. At this unique juncture, the energy of the water molecules is balanced in such a way that they can freely transition between being part of a solid, liquid, or gas. This delicate equilibrium provides a fascinating glimpse into the phase transitions of matter and is a critical concept in thermodynamics and physical chemistry. The triple point is not only a curiosity but also serves as a standard in defining the Kelvin temperature scale, highlighting its scientific significance.

Interesting Tidbit:

The triple point concept isn't exclusive to water; it applies to all pure substances, though the specific conditions vary for each. For instance, carbon dioxide's triple point occurs at about -56.6 degrees Celsius, which is why CO2 goes directly from a solid (dry ice) to a gas at atmospheric pressure, a process known as sublimation.

Fact #7: A Bridge Across Time

Cleopatra VII, the last active ruler of the Ptolemaic Kingdom of Egypt, is often envisioned amidst the ancient wonders of her time. Yet, a startling chronological fact brings her much closer to the modern era than the architectural marvels of early Egyptian civilization.

Cleopatra VII reigned from 51-30 BC, a period that seems to sit deeply in the annals of ancient history. However, when placed on a timeline, Cleopatra's life is significantly closer to the 1969 Moon landing than to the construction of the Great Pyramid of Giza, which was completed around 2560 BC. This means that the iconic pyramids were already about 2,500 years old by the time Cleopatra ascended to the throne. This perspective-shifting fact highlights the vast spans of time that separate significant events in human history, reminding us that ancient civilizations like Egypt had long and complex histories well before figures like Cleopatra came to the fore.

Interesting Tidbit:

Cleopatra's reign is closer in time to the invention of the smartphone than to the construction of the Great Pyramid. This further emphasizes the incredible depth of Egypt's history and the relatively compressed nature of modern technological advancements.

Fact #8: Predators Preceding Pines

Sharks, often viewed as timeless oceanic predators, have a lineage that predates even the earliest trees on Earth. This fact invites us to reconsider the age and evolution of life on our planet, showcasing the ancient origins of these marine creatures.

Sharks have been gliding through Earth's oceans for about 400 million years, making them one of the oldest living groups of animals on the planet. This incredible span of time means that sharks were already ancient swimmers when the first trees began to take root around 350 million years ago during the Devonian period. The survival of sharks through multiple mass extinctions and countless environmental changes speaks to their evolutionary success and adaptability. Unlike the solid, fossilizable bones of terrestrial animals, shark skeletons are made of cartilage, which is much less likely to fossilize, making their ancient history somewhat elusive but no less fascinating. The evolution of trees, on the other hand, marked a significant turning point in Earth's history, contributing to the development of land ecosystems and altering the planet's climate and atmosphere.

Interesting Tidbit:

The first trees, belonging to a group known as Archaeopteris, bore little resemblance to the trees we're familiar with today. These early plants were more akin to giant ferns with woody stems, and they played a crucial role in converting Earth's atmosphere by increasing oxygen levels and paving the way for terrestrial animals.

Fact #9: The Muffled Melody

Humming, a simple and universal form of musical expression, encounters an unexpected limitation when one tries to perform it while holding their nose. This intriguing fact sheds light on the interconnectedness of our bodily functions and the physics of sound production.

Humming is produced by the vibration of vocal cords and the resonant amplification of those vibrations within our body's cavities, particularly the nasal passages and mouth. When we hum, the sound largely exits through the nose, which acts as a resonating chamber. Clamping the nostrils shut blocks this passage, effectively stopping the sound from resonating properly and escaping, rendering us unable to hum in the traditional sense. This phenomenon highlights the importance of airflow in the production of certain sounds and serves as a practical demonstration of how our anatomy contributes to our ability to produce and modulate sound.

Interesting Tidbit:

This fact not only underscores the physics of sound but also hints at why certain singing techniques and vocal practices emphasize the role of nasal passages in achieving specific tonal qualities or resonance. Singers often use nasal resonance to enrich their tone or project their voice more effectively.

Fact #10: Flamboyance in Feathers

The English language is replete with unique and often whimsical terms for groups of animals, but few are as vividly descriptive as the term for a gathering of flamingos. Dubbed a "flamboyance," this term perfectly captures the striking appearance and behaviour of these vibrant birds.

Flamingos, with their brilliant pink feathers, stilt-like legs, and gregarious nature, are among the most easily recognizable and universally admired birds. The term "flamboyance" reflects not only the visual spectacle of a group of flamingos but also their behaviour, as they often perform synchronized movements in large groups, which can be quite a sight in their natural habitats. This social behaviour is crucial for flamingo life, aiding in everything from feeding to predator avoidance and even breeding rituals. The pink hue of their feathers, a result of their diet rich in beta-carotene from sources like algae and shrimp, further adds to the flamboyant display, making a gathering of flamingos one of the most visually captivating sights in the animal kingdom.

Interesting Tidbit:

The colour intensity of a flamingo's feathers can indicate its health and dietary status, serving as a signal to potential mates. A more vibrantly coloured flamingo is often healthier and has a better diet, making it a more desirable mate.

Fact #11: The Unseen Hazard

In a surprising twist on perceived dangers, vending machines, mundane fixtures of modern life, present a greater risk to human safety than the much-feared sharks. This fact challenges our perceptions of risk and highlights the unexpected dangers in everyday environments.

Statistically, vending machines cause more fatalities annually than shark attacks. The primary risk arises not from malfunctions or electrical faults but from individuals attempting to tilt or shake the machines to retrieve stuck items or to cheat the system. These actions can cause the machines, which often weigh several hundred pounds, to tip over, leading to serious injuries or even fatalities. In contrast, shark attacks are exceedingly rare and often less fatal than popular culture might suggest. This stark comparison between the two hazards serves as a poignant reminder of the often-misplaced focus of our fears, urging a reassessment of what we consider to be everyday risks.

Interesting Tidbit:

Efforts have been made to make vending machines safer, including warning labels and the implementation of tilt sensors that trigger an alarm or shut down the machine. Despite these measures, the best safety advice is to use vending machines as intended and report any issues to the responsible authorities.

Fact #12: Westward from the Coast

Geography often holds surprises that challenge our intuitive understanding of direction and location. A case in point is the unexpected geographic truth that Reno, Nevada, a city well inland, lies west of Los Angeles, California, which borders the Pacific Ocean.

The positioning of Reno and Los Angeles on the map defies common expectations. Los Angeles, situated on the southwestern coast of the United States, is known for its vast coastal line along the Pacific Ocean. Meanwhile, Reno is located near the western border of Nevada, adjacent to California. However, due to the curvature of the state boundaries and the coastal line, Reno is actually positioned west of Los Angeles when viewed on a longitude map. This geographical oddity serves as a fascinating example of how state lines and natural topography can lead to counterintuitive truths, reminding us that our mental maps of places are not always as accurate as we might believe.

Interesting Tidbit:

This fact is often used as a fun piece of trivia to illustrate the complex and sometimes unexpected nature of geography, highlighting that assumptions based on general knowledge of a region's layout might not always hold true when examined more closely.

Fact #13: Cosmic Abundance

The vastness of the universe is often difficult to comprehend, but comparing the number of stars in the cosmos to something as tangible as grains of sand on Earth's beaches can provide a glimpse into the infinite expanse of space.

Astronomers estimate that there are about 1×10^{24} stars in the observable universe, a figure that dwarfs the estimated number of grains of sand on all of Earth's beaches, which is around 7.5×10^{18}. This comparison not only highlights the sheer scale of the cosmos but also serves as a humbling reminder of our place within it. Each grain of sand represents a star, many of which could have their own system of planets, potentially teeming with life. The thought that for every grain of sand there are over a hundred stars puts into perspective the possibilities of the universe and the ongoing quest for knowledge in astronomy.

Interesting Tidbit:

While this fact is a compelling illustration of the universe's vastness, it's also a testament to the power of scientific estimation and the methods astronomers use to gauge the incomprehensible scale of the cosmos, from the observable local group of galaxies to the furthest reaches of the observable universe.

Fact #14: The Weight of a Star in Your Hand

Neutron stars, the dense remnants of supernova explosions, defy common perceptions of density and weight, encapsulating the mass of the Sun within a city-sized sphere. This fact about the weight of neutron star material brings the extreme conditions of the universe into stark relief.

A neutron star is formed from the collapsed core of a massive star after a supernova explosion. In this process, protons and electrons merge to form neutrons, resulting in an incredibly dense object. Just a teaspoon of neutron star material would weigh approximately 6 billion tons, akin to compressing the entire human population into a space smaller than a sugar cube. This unimaginable density is a consequence of the star's gravity crushing atoms until their nuclei are tightly packed together, with no empty space between them. The concept challenges our everyday experiences with gravity and density, providing a glimpse into the extraordinary conditions that exist beyond our planet.

Interesting Tidbit:

Despite their small size, neutron stars are incredibly massive and have a gravitational field so strong that if you were to drop an object from just one meter above its surface, it would hit the neutron star in just one microsecond, reaching speeds of around 7 million kilometres per hour.

Fact #15: An Ancient Seat of Learning

The timeline of human civilization is filled with surprising juxtapositions that challenge our linear perceptions of history. The existence of Oxford University, a venerable institution of learning, predating the rise of the Aztec Empire in the Americas, is one such intriguing historical overlap.

Oxford University, with its origins dating back to at least the 12th century, stands as one of the oldest continuously operating universities in the world. Its foundation predates the establishment of the Aztec Empire in the early 14th century, around 1325, when the Aztec people founded the city of Tenochtitlán, which is now Mexico City. This fact illuminates the asynchronous development of civilizations and cultures across different continents. While Oxford was already a flourishing centre of learning and scholarship in Europe, across the ocean, the Aztecs were laying the foundations for what would become one of the most sophisticated civilizations in the Americas, known for its architectural, mathematical, and astronomical achievements.

Interesting Tidbit:

The Aztec Empire, despite its later start, quickly grew into a powerful entity known for its complex social structure, economy, and impressive accomplishments in engineering and the arts. Meanwhile, Oxford University was establishing itself as a beacon of education, influencing the course of Western thought and scholarship for centuries to come.

Fact #16: The Sleeping Sneeze Conundrum

Sneezing, a reflex triggered by irritants in the nasal passage, is a familiar, involuntary response. However, this seemingly unstoppable reaction has its limits, particularly in the realm of sleep, revealing fascinating aspects of how our body regulates reflexes.

During sleep, particularly in the rapid eye movement (REM) phase, our body enters a state of muscle atonia, where most of the skeletal muscles are paralyzed, including those involved in the sneeze reflex. This temporary paralysis is the brain's way of preventing us from acting out our dreams. Moreover, the sneeze reflex is largely suppressed while we sleep, due to the decreased sensitivity of the mucous membranes to irritants and a general reduction in airflow through the nose. This suppression is part of a broader downregulation of many reflexes by the brain to maintain uninterrupted sleep and protect the body from unnecessary disturbances.

Interesting Tidbit:

While it's highly unlikely to sneeze in your sleep, if a strong enough irritant is present, it might wake you up just enough to trigger a sneeze, although you're more likely to sneeze upon waking than while deeply asleep.

Fact #17: Alaska's Geographic Extremes

Alaska, the largest U.S. state by area, is often associated with its northern extremities. However, its unique position on the globe grants it the distinction of being the most northern, eastern, and western state in the United States, challenging conventional perceptions of geography.

Alaska's northernmost point is well-known, but its status as the easternmost and westernmost state might seem counterintuitive at first glance. This is due to the Aleutian Islands, which stretch out into the Bering Sea and cross the 180th meridian, the generally accepted dividing line between the Eastern and Western Hemispheres. Thus, the Aleutian Islands extend Alaska's reach into the Eastern Hemisphere, making it the only U.S. state to occupy both hemispheres. This unique geographic feature highlights the arbitrary nature of longitudinal divisions and the interesting quirks they can produce in territorial delineations.

Interesting Tidbit:

The 180th meridian, where Alaska stretches into the Eastern Hemisphere, is also closely associated with the International Date Line, although the line zigzags to avoid dividing countries and territories. This results in some of the Aleutian Islands being a day ahead of the rest of the United States, adding another layer of intrigue to Alaska's geographical distinctions.

Fact #18: Pluto's Long Journey

Pluto, once considered the ninth planet in our solar system, has a peculiar story not just in terms of its planetary status but also its slow journey around the Sun. Its orbit is so lengthy that it hadn't completed a full orbit since its discovery before being reclassified as a dwarf planet.

Discovered in 1930, Pluto was regarded as the ninth planet in the solar system until 2006, when the International Astronomical Union (IAU) redefined what constitutes a planet, leading to Pluto's reclassification as a dwarf planet. One of the most fascinating aspects of Pluto's story is its orbital period around the Sun, which takes about 248 Earth years. This means that from the time of its discovery to its demotion, Pluto had not completed a full orbit around the Sun. This fact not only highlights the vast distances and timescales involved in our solar system but also serves as a poignant reminder of the ever-evolving nature of scientific understanding and classification.

Interesting Tidbit:

Pluto's orbit is highly eccentric, meaning it's not a perfect circle but rather an elongated oval. This eccentricity leads to Pluto being closer to the Sun than Neptune for about 20 years of its orbit, challenging the notion of a neatly ordered solar system.

Fact #19: The Immortal Jellyfish

Among the myriad of life forms on Earth, one species stands out for its defiance of life's ultimate certainty: death. The Turritopsis dohrnii, often called the "immortal jellyfish," possesses a unique ability to revert back to its juvenile form after reaching maturity, a phenomenon that challenges our understanding of biological aging and mortality.

The Turritopsis dohrnii, a small species of jellyfish found in temperate to tropical regions, has captivated scientists with its seemingly endless lifecycle. Upon reaching maturity or encountering environmental stress, physical harm, or scarcity of food, this jellyfish can undergo a process known as transdifferentiation. This process allows its cells to transform into different types of cells, effectively allowing the jellyfish to revert to its polyp stage, the earliest point in its life cycle. This ability to cycle from maturity back to infancy, potentially indefinitely, grants it a form of biological immortality, although it remains susceptible to disease and predation.

Interesting Tidbit:

This remarkable survival strategy is currently the subject of extensive research, as understanding the mechanisms behind the Turritopsis dohrnii's regenerative process could have profound implications for medicine, particularly in the fields of aging and cellular regeneration.

Fact #20: Geometric Excretions

In the annals of the animal kingdom, where wonders never cease, the humble wombat contributes an oddity that seems more at home in a geometry class than in the wild: cube-shaped poop. This peculiar characteristic of wombat feces is not only a curiosity but also an adaptation that speaks volumes about the intersection of biology and physics.

Wombats, native to Australia, are the only known animals capable of producing cube-shaped feces. This unusual shape is the result of the wombat's extraordinarily long and slow digestive process, which can take up to two weeks, allowing the intestines to extract nutrients and shape the feces into cubes. The final shaping occurs in the last sections of the intestine, where the feces develop their flat sides and sharp edges. Scientists believe this cubic form serves a practical purpose: it prevents the droppings from rolling away, enabling wombats to mark their territory and communicate through scent more effectively, especially in their rocky and hilly habitats.

Interesting Tidbit:

The wombat's unique digestive process has piqued the interest of scientists and engineers alike. Studies of wombat intestines have revealed that the cube shapes are formed by the elasticity of the intestinal walls, which contract unevenly. This natural engineering marvel has potential applications in manufacturing and cube-shaped product creation, showcasing once again how nature can inspire technological innovation.

Fact #21: A Brief Battle

History is filled with protracted conflicts that have shaped the course of nations, but not all wars have been lengthy affairs. The Anglo-Zanzibar War stands out for its brevity, earning the distinction of being the shortest war in recorded history.

The conflict between Britain and the Sultanate of Zanzibar on August 27, 1896, was precipitated by the death of the pro-British Sultan Hamad bin Thuwaini and the subsequent succession by Sultan Khalid bin Barghash, who was less favourable to British interests. The British authorities issued an ultimatum to Sultan Khalid to step down, which he defied, leading to a military confrontation. The British naval forces bombarded the Sultan's palace, and within 38 minutes, the Sultan's defences were overwhelmed, and a ceasefire was declared. Sultan Khalid sought refuge in the German consulate and was later exiled, marking a swift end to the hostilities. This short-lived war underscored the extent of British influence and power in the region during that era.

Interesting Tidbit:

Despite its short duration, the war had significant implications for Zanzibar, leading to the installation of a more compliant Sultan and further solidifying British influence in the region. The quick resolution also demonstrated the military capabilities and global reach of the British Empire at the time.

Fact #22: The Heavyweight in the Sky

Clouds, those ethereal, fluffy masses floating in the sky, belie a surprising heft. Despite their seemingly weightless appearance, the water content in a cloud can give it a staggering weight, challenging our perceptions of the natural world.

A typical cumulus cloud, which appears light and cottony, is anything but insubstantial. Scientists estimate that an average cumulus cloud, which might be about a cubic kilometre in size, can hold approximately 1.1 million pounds (about 500,000 kilograms) of water. This immense weight is supported by the atmosphere, where temperature variations and updrafts keep the water droplets (and ice crystals at higher altitudes) suspended in the air. The cloud's weight is dispersed over such a vast area and is made up of tiny water droplets that it remains afloat and doesn't come crashing down on us.

Interesting Tidbit:

The water content of a cloud is distributed across a vast number of droplets. In fact, a typical cumulus cloud can contain around 500 million litres of water, distributed across trillions of water droplets, each of which is so small that it takes about a million of them to form a single raindrop.

Fact #23: A Crowded Circle

In an illustration of the dense population distribution in certain parts of the world, a seemingly arbitrary circle drawn on the globe encompasses more human lives than the entire area outside it, offering a stark visualization of global population density.

A geographical curiosity arises when drawing a circle on the world map that includes parts of Eastern China, Southeast Asia, the Indian subcontinent, and the surrounding areas. Despite covering a relatively small fraction of the Earth's total surface area, this region is home to more than half of the world's population. The circle might pass through countries like China, India, Indonesia, Pakistan, Bangladesh, and Japan, among others. This concentration highlights the significant population densities in these areas, driven by factors such as fertile land, favourable climates, and historical development patterns. It's a compelling way to visualize how human populations are distributed across the planet and the vast differences in population density from one region to another.

Interesting Tidbit:

This fact often surprises people, as it challenges common perceptions about the distribution of land and people. For instance, countries like China and India each have populations exceeding 1 billion, significantly contributing to the high population density within this circle.

Fact #24: A Tower That Grows

The Eiffel Tower, an iconic symbol of Paris, is not only an architectural marvel but also a subject of scientific interest due to its metal structure's reaction to temperature changes. This fact highlights the intriguing interplay between materials science and the changing seasons.

Metal expands when heated and contracts when cooled, a property known as thermal expansion. The Eiffel Tower, constructed primarily of iron, is subject to this physical principle. During the summer months, when temperatures rise, the metal in the tower expands, causing the entire structure to grow in height by up to 15 centimeters (about 6 inches). This subtle yet significant change is a testament to the tower's dynamic interaction with its environment, illustrating how even monumental structures are not immune to the laws of physics. The expansion is evenly distributed throughout the tower's structure, ensuring its integrity despite the slight increase in size.

Interesting Tidbit:

The tower's designer, Gustave Eiffel, ingeniously incorporated thermal expansion into its design, allowing the iron structure to flex without compromising its stability. This adaptability contributes to the tower's longevity and enduring appeal.

Fact #25: Precipitation of Precious Stones

Beyond the confines of Earth's familiar weather patterns lies a phenomenon in the outer solar system that seems straight out of a fantasy. On the gas giants Saturn and Jupiter, the atmospheric conditions are such that it literally rains diamonds, a fact that ignites the imagination with visions of celestial wealth.

The atmospheres of Saturn and Jupiter are rich in methane gas. When storms occur on these planets, lightning strikes convert methane into soot (carbon), which as it falls deeper into the atmosphere, undergoes immense pressure and heat, transforming first into graphite and then into diamond. These diamonds continue to fall through the atmosphere until they reach temperatures so high that they likely melt into a liquid form, creating a "diamond rain." This extraordinary process is a result of the intense atmospheric pressure and heat found on these gas giants, conditions vastly different from those on Earth. The concept of diamond rain adds a layer of marvel to the already fascinating nature of the outer planets, showcasing the diverse and extreme weather phenomena that can occur in our solar system.

Interesting Tidbit:

The amount of diamond rain on these planets is not trivial; scientists estimate that thousands of tons of diamonds could be produced annually on Saturn and Jupiter. This fact not only highlights the exotic weather patterns found on other planets but also challenges our Earth-centric perspectives on value and material wealth.

Fact #26: Just a Jiffy

"Jiffy" is commonly used in casual conversation to denote a very short amount of time, but few realize that it is also a bona fide scientific term with precise definitions in different contexts, embodying the intersection between everyday language and scientific precision.

In the realm of physics and electronics, a jiffy is defined as the time it takes for light to travel one centimetre in a vacuum, approximately 33.3564 picoseconds (a picosecond is one trillionth of a second). This definition underscores the term's relevance in fields where precise measurements of very short time intervals are essential. The concept of a jiffy provides insight into the microscopic scale at which some scientific phenomena occur, offering a bridge between the colloquial use of the term and its practical applications in scientific research and technology.

Interesting Tidbit:

The term "jiffy" has different definitions depending on the scientific discipline. For example, in computing, a jiffy can refer to the duration of one tick of the system timer interrupt, which varies depending on the operating system and hardware. This variability reflects the term's flexibility and its adaptation to specific contexts within the scientific community.

Fact #27: Momentary Distinction

Within the intricate mosaic of human existence, where fleeting moments merge into the endless flow of time, the birth of each person marks a brief moment of distinction. This fact illuminates the transient reality of being the planet's youngest person, a title each of us possesses for a mere instant.

With babies being born at a rate of several per second around the world, the title of "the youngest person on Earth" is in constant flux. At the exact moment of your birth, you held this distinction, even if it was only for a fraction of a second, before another birth occurred and passed the title on. This realization serves as a poignant reminder of the shared beginnings of all human life, highlighting the interconnectedness and continuous cycle of birth that characterizes our species. It's a unifying fact that every person, regardless of where they end up in life, started at exactly the same point: as the newest addition to humanity.

Interesting Tidbit:

The continuous cycle of birth and the rapid succession of "youngest person" titles underscore the dynamic and ever-changing nature of the human population. It also reflects the statistical and probabilistic nature of life events, where individual experiences are woven into the broader fabric of human existence.

Fact #28: The Mpemba Paradox

The Mpemba effect, a counterintuitive phenomenon where hot water can freeze faster than cold water under certain conditions, challenges our basic understanding of thermodynamics and continues to puzzle scientists and laypeople alike.

Initially observed by Erasto Mpemba in Tanzania in the 1960s, this effect has been subject to various studies, yet no single explanation has been universally accepted. Several factors are thought to contribute to the Mpemba effect, including evaporation (which reduces the volume of hot water, allowing it to freeze more quickly), convection (leading to a more uniform cooling of the hot water), and the properties of water molecules themselves. The Mpemba effect serves as a fascinating reminder of the complexities of physical phenomena and the potential for exceptions to conventional rules in the natural world.

Interesting Tidbit:

The Mpemba effect has been known in various cultures and throughout history, with references dating back to Aristotle, who observed that "warm water freezes more quickly than cold." However, it wasn't until Mpemba's observations in the 20th century that the phenomenon began to be studied more systematically.

Fact #29: Bovine Bonds

The emotional lives of animals continue to be a rich area of discovery, revealing complexities that resonate with human experiences. Among these findings is the heartwarming fact that cows form close friendships within their herds, demonstrating preferences for certain companions, akin to having a "best friend."

Research in animal behaviour has shown that cows are social creatures that establish significant bonds with specific individuals in their herd. These bonds are characterized by spending a considerable amount of time together, showing signs of distress when separated. Cows with their preferred companions exhibit lower stress levels, as indicated by their heart rates and behaviours, compared to when they are with unfamiliar peers. This social bonding is essential for their overall well-being, highlighting the importance of social structures and relationships in the animal kingdom.

Interesting Tidbit:

The understanding of such social bonds in cows not only sheds light on the emotional depth of animals but also has practical implications for how herds are managed in farming practices. Recognizing and accommodating the social needs of cows can lead to healthier and more content herds, with benefits for their welfare and productivity.

Fact #30: Scotland's Mythical Emblem

National animals are often chosen for their traits, symbolism, or prevalence within a country. Scotland, however, stands out for its selection of a mythical creature, the unicorn, as its national animal, a choice that reflects the country's rich folklore and love for the mystical.

The unicorn, a symbol of purity, innocence, and power in Celtic mythology, has been associated with Scotland for centuries. Its presence is woven into the country's history and heraldry, signifying strength and purity. The choice of such a mythical creature highlights the deep-rooted cultural significance and the value placed on ideals and virtues over physical attributes. The unicorn is often depicted in chains, representing the belief that a free unicorn was a dangerous and fierce creature, yet could be tamed by a virgin – a metaphor for the power of innocence and purity.

Interesting Tidbit:

The unicorn has been a Scottish heraldic symbol since the 12th century. When King James VI of Scotland also became James I of England, the Scottish Royal Arms featured two unicorns. However, post-union, one unicorn was replaced by a lion (the national animal of England) to symbolize the unity between the two countries.

Fact #31: The Nine-Brained Marvel

The octopus, a creature renowned for its intelligence and adaptability, possesses a fascinating neurological structure that sets it apart from most other life forms: a central brain and a unique complement of eight additional "brains."

An octopus's central brain controls its nervous system, while each of its eight arms contains a smaller, ganglion-like brain that allows for remarkable control and sensory perception. This decentralized nervous system enables the arms to operate semi-independently, coordinating complex movements and tactile exploration without direct oversight from the central brain. This arrangement is particularly advantageous given the octopus's habitat and lifestyle, which demand high levels of spatial awareness, dexterity, and problem-solving abilities. The autonomy of each arm allows the octopus to perform multiple tasks simultaneously, from navigating rocky crevices to manipulating objects and hunting.

Interesting Tidbit:

This neural arrangement not only contributes to the octopus's survival and adaptability but also poses intriguing questions about the nature of consciousness and intelligence. Studies have shown that octopus arms can execute simple tasks even when disassociated from the body, demonstrating a level of autonomy that challenges our traditional understanding of brain-body coordination.

Fact #32: Sparks Before Strikes

In the timeline of human innovation, the development of tools for creating fire marks significant milestones. Contrary to what one might expect, the portable mechanical lighter was invented before the friction match, an interesting twist in the history of technology.

The first mechanical lighter, known as the "Döbereiner's lamp," was invented in 1823 by Johann Wolfgang Döbereiner, a German chemist. This device used a reaction between hydrogen and a platinum catalyst to produce a flame. It was a significant innovation of its time, offering a portable means to create fire. In contrast, the first successful friction match was invented by John Walker, an English chemist, in 1826, three years after the lighter. Walker's friction matches, which ignited when struck against a rough surface, became widely used because they were cheaper and more convenient than the early lighters. The inversion of these inventions in the historical timeline challenges common assumptions about the progression of technological innovation.

Interesting Tidbit:

Döbereiner's lighter was a table-top device rather than the pocket-sized lighters we're familiar with today. Its invention not only predates the friction match but also sparked (pun intended) further innovations in the field of portable fire-starting tools, leading to the development of more practical and compact lighters over time.

Fact #33: Tasteful Steps

The natural world is replete with wonders that often defy human expectations, one of which is the remarkable sensory adaptation found in butterflies. These delicate insects, known for their vibrant colors and graceful flight, possess the unique ability to taste with their feet, a feature that underscores the diversity of sensory perception in the animal kingdom.

Butterflies have taste receptors located on their feet, allowing them to detect the suitability of a plant for laying eggs as soon as they land on it. This sensory adaptation is crucial for their survival, enabling them to find the right host plants for their offspring to feed on once hatched. The taste receptors, known as chemosensors, can instantly assess the chemical composition of the plant, ensuring that the butterfly's larvae will have the appropriate nourishment to grow and develop. This fascinating aspect of butterfly biology highlights the intricate relationships between species and their environments, showcasing the evolutionary innovations that enable life to thrive in diverse ecosystems.

Interesting Tidbit:

This ability to "taste" with their feet is not only practical for survival but also serves as a vivid example of how different life forms have evolved unique mechanisms to interact with their surroundings. It invites us to consider the myriad ways in which organisms perceive the world, often in manners vastly different from human sensory experiences.

As we draw the curtain on this journey through the corridors of the curious and the extraordinary, I, Alex Wright, extend my heartfelt gratitude to you, dear reader, for embarking on this voyage of discovery with me. Your curiosity and thirst for knowledge have been the true compass guiding this exploration of facts that dance on the edge of believability.

In the pages of this book, we've traversed time and space, delved into the marvels of the natural world, and uncovered the quirky underpinnings of our universe. It is my sincere hope that this collection has not only entertained but also ignited a spark of wonder within you—a reminder that the world is replete with mysteries waiting to be uncovered.

A special thank you is also due to the myriad of researchers, scientists, and storytellers whose work has paved the way for the tales told within these covers. Their relentless pursuit of understanding and their dedication to unraveling the fabric of our reality are what make compilations like this possible.

Disclaimer:

While every effort has been made to ensure the accuracy and reliability of the information presented in this book, the dynamic nature of scientific discovery means that our understanding of the universe and its many wonders is constantly evolving. As such, I invite readers to approach these pages with both an open mind and a healthy dose of skepticism, always ready to explore further and question deeper.

In closing, I thank you once more for your companionship on this journey. May your path be ever illuminated by the light of curiosity, and may the world never cease to amaze you.

With deepest appreciation,
Alex Wright

www.ingramcontent.com/pod-product-compliance
Lightning Source LLC
Chambersburg PA
CBHW051845250726
48659CB00006B/2030